Herb Gardening

LOUISE HARVEY

ISBN-13: 978-1514676899
ISBN-10: 1514676893

CONTENTS

INTRODUCTION TO HERBS

If there was one thing that really got me thinking about starting my own garden it was my love of fresh herbs.

What can be better than taking some herbs from your garden and using it in a dish you have prepared? Fresh herbs add so much to cooking. Firstly, I love their color, so bright and alive. Secondly, they are filled with flavor and thirdly, they are rich in antioxidants and nutrients essential to our bodies.

Over the years I have also learnt that herbs can be used for so many other things as well. Peppermint leaves are great to help ease coughs and fight colds, while thyme has so many uses that I always forget most of them, however, I use it as in indoor insect repellant. Flies and mosquitos hate it!

My aim with this eBook is to help you to grow your own herbs. We will discuss 10 different herbs and look at how each can be used, how to grow them, how to cultivate them and how to store them. Finally, I will give you a few of my favorite uses of each herb in the kitchen and other ways in which they can be used.

I really hope you enjoy reading this eBook. Take your time, there will be plenty of information to get through, but at the end of it, you will know exactly which herbs you want to grow in your herb garden.

WHY GROW HERBS AT HOME?

Mankind has been using herbs since the dawn of time. Of course, initially herbs were never really used in cooking, but more in a medicinal capacity.

One of the earliest records of herbs used in a medicinal way can be found from on ancient papyrus, called the Papyrus Ebers. This document was discovered in 1884 by German archaeologist, George Ebers. It is thought the Papyrus itself dates from around 1500BC, although all indications are that it is a copy of an earlier document, proving the Egyptians used medicinal herbs even before this. The scroll itself is over 20 meters long and contains 700 remedies which use plants and herbs as their main ingredients.

The ancient Chinese performed their own herbal study in around 2000BC. This was conducted by the emperor of the time, Shen Nong and took the form of a manuscript called Shennong Bencaojing. It includes uses for herbs in medicine and over 300 plants are included.

Greek and Roman societies also used herbs, mostly for medicinal purposes but they also had a few other novel applications. The Greeks smeared themselves with bruised mint leaves after taking a bath while the Romans used dill as a fragrance in rooms. Herbs have been used by just about every civilization through the ages!

But why should we grow them at home? Well I have a number of reasons I think herbs are a perfect addition to any garden.

- **Herbs are easy to grow!**

  Herbs really are extremely versatile in this regard. They can be grown in the garden, in window boxes or even as a small pot plant. What is better than choosing herbs straight from your window sill in your kitchen and adding them to your cooking?

Herbs also thrive when they are repeatedly harvested.

I actually grow my herbs in two ways. Firstly, I have a designated area in my back garden and secondly I keep a few of my favorite herbs in my kitchen ready for use!

- **Using fresh herbs is more beneficial than buying them**

  Did you know that more than half the nutritional value of a plant or herb is lost in the first 30 minutes after it is harvested? Well, if you have fresh herbs in your garden you will not lose any of their antioxidants or nutrients as you will, in all likelihood, use them straight after you harvest them.

- **Using fresh herbs is more beneficial than buying them**

  Do you buy herbs from your local store and end up throwing half of them away? I am not sure why they are packed in such large amounts as herbs are packed with flavor and only a little goes a long way. When you have your own herb garden you only use what you need. This means less waste and more money saved, a good thing in my book!

- **Stress relief**

  Gardening in general is a great stress reliever, but spending time in your herb garden in particular, is really the best way to relax. I just love the different fragrances of each plant. In fact, when I am feeling a little overwhelmed, my herb garden is the first place I head for.

- **Herbs are beautiful!**

  Another of my favorite reasons to grow herbs! They are so beautiful, come in so many varieties, textures and colors. They really just add an extra dimension to any garden.

8

BASIL

If I had to pick a favorite herb, it would have to be basil. It comes in so many varieties, but I love the good old traditional sweet basil and those big, green leaves, filled with flavor. As you begin to tear the leaves apart, you can smell exactly how they taste. In fact, I often pop a basil leaf in my mouth and just chew away!

It is thought that basil comes from India, an area where it has been grown for a many thousands of years. There are many versions of the plant, the most well-known arc sweet basil, purple basil and Thai basil.

A sweet basil plant (the most common variety) consists of large, round, dark green leaves, which often have a slightly pointed tip. The plant is very bushy in appearance and grow to around 2 feet high at their largest.

How to grow basil

Growing a basil plant is relatively simple. As with all plants, you will need to keep a control of light, water, soil, temperature as well as feeding the plant. Let's look at each aspect a little more closely.

- **Light**

    Basil plants do not mind full sun at all. In fact, they will require a fair share of light to grow to their full potential. If you are growing a basil plant indoors, try to ensure it is in an area that receives close to 8 hours of sunlight a day.

    Can a basil plant get too much sun? Yes it can! Always check the leaves of your plant and if you notice them starting to go yellow and wilt, it is probably getting too much sun. Move it to a different location and see if it recovers. Of course, you may just not be giving it enough water but we will get into that a bit later.

9

I like my basil plants to get the early morning sun followed by some afternoon shade. It seems to work very well for them.

- **Water**

Basil plants have very basic watering requirements. Of course, you need to get the balancing act as accurate as possible and this depends on the climate in which the plant is grown. That said, a basil plant should never be allowed to dry out. I like to check mine daily by placing my index finger into the soil to around an inch deep. If it is dry, the plant needs to be watered. This method can be used on indoor and outdoor plants and I use it for all my herbs.

For indoor plants, use tepid water and also make sure the pots have drainage holes. Water near the stem, do not water the leaves. If the plant has smaller leaves near the base of the stem, be sure to move them out the way. Let the plant drain thoroughly after watering and never let it sit in any excess water. This can cause mildew and attract various fungi which will attack the plant.

For outdoor plants, drainage is just as important. The plant must not be left in any standing water that cannot drain away. This will cause mildew and attract fungus. If you are unsure if your plant needs water, consider purchasing a soil moisture meter. This can help prevent against both overwatering as well as drying the ground out too much.

- **Soil**

When it comes to the best type of soil for a basil plant, you require something that will drain efficiently.

For indoor basil, I prefer using a soilless mix consisting of equal parts peat and aged bark. The advantage of this mix is that it drains really well. Another option that has been recommended to me are sphagnum, wood chip and perlite mixed in equal parts.

There is little you can do for plants that are growing outside, unless you want to resoil the entire bed where your basil grows. A loamy soil is often best for basil growing outside.

- **Temperature**

Basil thrives in temperatures of around 70 degrees Fahrenheit, but be warned, the plant does not like the cold at all. Outdoor plants exposed to frost will die.

- **Feeding**

Basil can be fertilized but it is quite a balancing act. Indoor plants should be fed at intervals of every four to six weeks while those growing outdoors should be fed more regularly. I like to feed my outdoor plants at least every two to three weeks.

Basil requires fertilizers containing nitrogen, potassium and phosphorus. A 10-10-10 mix at half strength stimulates all round plant growth. Bigger leaves can be achieved with a higher nitrogen content, although I have found that this does impact in a negative way on flavor of the leaves. You can either use a liquid fertilizer or granules. If you do use granules make sure that they dissolve properly and penetrate into the soil.

Pruning and harvesting basil

I have found that by pruning my basil plants they remain healthy and continue to produce many excellent leaves. Indoor plants often need to be repotted and this is the best time to prune them. I normally cut them above their second grouping of leaves. Thereafter, I prune plants to around 1/3 of their size every three to four weeks. Sweet basil is an annual and it should never be allowed to flower. This will mark the end of the life cycle of the plant but by cutting the flower pods off before flowering, the cycle can be extended. Flowering also affects the taste of the leaves making them slightly bitter.

When harvesting basil I prefer to pick the leaves in the morning. I think the leaves have more flavor then. However, there is no harm in taking leaves from your basil plant whenever you need them.

Preserving and storing basil

Basil can be dried but I much prefer fresh basil over the dried version. Having said that, you might have so much basil leaves you do not know what to do with them.

There are a few methods in which basil can be dried. For the first method take bunches of leaves and leave them hanging in a cool, dry place. The leaves will dry out over time and can be crumbled into a powder. The second method requires a little more work on your part. Place single basil leaves in between a folded sheet of newspaper. Place the paper on a wire rack and turn the leaves at least on two occasions each day. After the leaves have dried, crumble into a powder and store in an air tight container in a cupboard. The basil should keep for up to a year. You could also add the crushed leaves to salt turning it into a delicious basil salt.

Basil can also be kept in a freezer although the leaves can sometimes blacken. To overcome this chop up the leaves, cover with a thin coating of oil and place the basil in a freezer bag. One of my favorite ways to keep basil is to chop it finely, add to oil and freeze in some ice trays – a perfect way to start off your cooking. Another great way to use basil is to make it into pesto.

Using basil in cooking

Basil is an incredibly versatile herb which can be used in numerous ways in the kitchen. It can be added to salads, soups, fish, meat, chicken and vegetables. It can also be used in combination with various other herbs especially garlic, rosemary, sage and thyme. Basil also goes well with any tomato based dishes.

Perhaps one of the best uses of basil is to make a pesto. There are numerous types of pesto but I am going to give you a basic recipe for one that I like to make. You will need the following ingredients.

- Chopped garlic (5 cloves)
- Pine nuts (¼ cup)
- Basil (4 cups)
- A pinch of salt
- Grated parmesan (½ cup)
- Extra-virgin olive oil (¾ cup)

This pesto can be made in a food processer or with a mortar and pestle. I like shortcuts, so I prefer to use a food processor. Take the garlic, pine nuts, basil, a pinch of salt and two tablespoons of olive oil, add them to the food processor and blitz till they are completely combined. Now add the parmesan and the left-over oil. Begin by pulse blitzing the ingredients and eventually process until the mixture becomes smooth and all ingredients are chopped up finely. Check the seasoning, adding if necessary.

Other uses for basil

Basil has many other uses not related to cooking. These include:

- Basil can help fight indigestion. You can eat a basil leaf or add ½ teaspoon of dried basil to some water and drink.
- Basil can help stop coughing. If you are coughing, basil can bring some relief. Pour some boiling water over a handful of basil leaves. Let the oils and flavor from the leaves draw into the water and drink.

- Basil can fight headaches. Steam yourself by adding a tablespoon of dried basil to around 2 cups of water. Place in a large container, cover your head with a towel and breathe in the steam rising from the container for around 10 minutes or until the headache subsides.

- Basil can stop itchiness from insect bites. If you have been bitten by an insect, chew on a basil leaf and then apply it to the area to remove any itchiness.

- Basil can help to reduce stress. Add 2 cups of a basil tea infusion to your hot bath. It will help you to relax and distress.

CHIVES

Chives are members of the lily family and come in a number of varieties, the most common are onion and garlic (Chinese) chives. They can be used in many forms of cooking or in salads, which is my favorite way to use them. Chives are a perennial plant.

The chive plant forms a very small bulb which stays under the ground as they grow. The stems of the herb can grow up to 20 inches tall but are only around ½ inch wide. These stems grow in thick bundles from near the root bulb of the plant. Chives produce beautiful purple flowers which are shaped in the form of a star.

How to grow chives

Chives are fairly easy to grow, both indoors and outdoors. You will need to control some variables such as light, water, soil, temperature as well as feeding the plant. Let's look at each aspect a little more closely.

- **Light**

    Indoor chive plants will require a fair amount of light so try to place them in an area where they will receive some sunlight. They can grow under fluorescent light as well, but I tend to keep mine in pots near windows so they are near natural light. If you are growing them outdoors, chives can be placed in full sun. Much like basil, I prefer my chives to receive less powerful morning sun coupled with some shade during the day.

    If you live in an area with very harsh sun conditions and high temperatures, check your chives regularly to ensure they are not getting too much sun.

- **Water**

Chives do not have any specific watering needs other than do not let the plant go thirsty! Always check the top inch of the soil they are growing in to determine if they need water or not. If it is dry, you should water the plant.

Indoor chives can be misted every now and again, especially if you live in an area very low humidity. As with basil, water must be allowed to drain away properly otherwise the bulb of the chive can rot.

The easiest way to water a chive plant is to soak the soil completely with tepid water and then let it drain thoroughly. Indoor chive plants should be kept in containers or pots with drainage holes. Chives can be watered fairly frequently as they grow but as they mature, they require less water.

- **Soil**

  Chives grow equally well in either a sandy or loamy soil but they will benefit from an organic compost mixed which has been mixed through it. As mentioned, the soil should drain easily at all times but have the ability to retain some moisture.

- **Temperature**

  Chives can grow in a broad temperature range. A colder climate will however stunt the rate at which the plant grows, sometimes only leaving bulbs below the ground. They will begin to grown again as the warmer weather sets in.

- **Feeding**

  Chive plants enjoy some fertilizer from time to time, especially if grown in less than ideal soil. A 20-20-20 of nitrogen, potassium and phosphorus can be used. Never use fertilizer with a higher nitrogen balance.

Use either a liquid or granule fertilizer, but if you are using granules, make sure to work them into the soil and that they dissolve properly.

Pruning and harvesting chives

As the plant grows it can be harvested by cutting it around 2 inches above the soil. I like to start with the leaves on the outside first, gradually moving my way inward.

I also like to harvest my chives when they reach around 6 inches in length as I have found that this really promotes growth. Your chives will flower from time to time. I tend to leave the flowers on as they are very pretty, but you can take the buds off as that will encourage even more growth out of your chives.

Once the flowers have bloomed and die, cut the stems right back.

Preserving and storing chives

Chives cannot be dried as they will lose all their flavors. You can freeze them and use them at a later date however. There are numerous ways to do this. Chop the chives and place them in a freezer bag or add them to water and fill up ice trays and freeze. Once frozen, remove from the tray and place in freezer bag. These are now perfect to add to soups or even sauces.

Using chives in cooking

My favorite way to use chives is in their raw form. They are great way to add a little onion or garlic zing to salads. Chives can also be used in soups, salads, egg dishes and added to vegetables.

The herb also makes an excellent herb butter. Here is a very basic recipe that I like to use. You will need the following ingredients.

- Softened unsalted butter (2 sticks)

- Snipped chives (¼ cup)
- Lemon zest (2 teaspoons)
- Salt and freshly ground pepper
- Garlic powder (¼ teaspoon)

Begin by combining all these ingredients together in a large mixing bowl. Once thoroughly combined, roll into a cylinder and place on plastic wrap. Roll until tight. Your butter is now ready. Keep it in the fridge and use when needed!

Other uses for chives

Chives can be used in a number of interesting ways.

- Chives are a natural pest repellent. Aphids in particular hate chive plants, so placing them near other plants susceptible to these pests can help protect them.
- Chives can also protect other plants from mildew. Boils some chives in water, add the cooled liquid to a spray bottle and spray your plants to help protect them.
- Chives have medicinal properties. Studies have shown that chives have anti-inflammatory, anti-bacterial and anti-viral properties. Regular consumption of this herb can lower the risk of a number of cancers as well as lower blood pressure.

DILL

Dill is thought to have originated in the Mediterranean region. It has long been used in many European cultures both in cooking and for medicinal purposes with records indicating its use in this regard around 3000 years ago. In Rome, gladiators were given meals with dill as it was believed it would grant both courage and valor.

Dill is an annual that can grow as high as 24 inches. It has a thin stem with alternate leaves growing from it. The leaves are very soft and are between 4 and 8 inches in length. The dill plant does flower, producing small white and yellow blossoms.

How to grow dill

You will need to take note of the following factors when growing dill.

- **Light**

  Dill loves full sunlight, but this coupled with hotter weather means a dill plant will flower. If you are growing the plant as a herb, you do not want it to flower as this will bring leaf production to an end. As with most of my other herbs in my garden, my dill plants receive morning sun coupled with some afternoon shade. This keeps them out of the harshest sun of the day.

  Dill can be grown indoors but it will require around 6 to 8 hours of natural sunlight per day so be sure to keep them near a window where they can receive this natural light.

- **Water**

  Dill is very delicate and it requires that you pay attention when watering. Try to add the water right at the base of the plant or dig small furrows in the soil and water into them. You do not want water to fall directly onto its stem as it can break. Trust me, I learned the hard way in this regard!

Never overwater dill as this can cause the plant to rot. Dill plants have fairly long roots that seek out water, but be sure to check the soil daily with your index finger. All indoor dill plants should be placed in pots with drainage holes so that excess water can drain away.

- **Soil**

  Dill is partial to soil between the light to medium textured range. The soil must provide excellent drainage but still remain moist so as to provide water for the plant. I often plant my dill in a soil enriched with organic compost, they seem to flourish fairly well in that.

- **Temperature**

  Dill prefers a mild temperature range. It thrives in areas where temperature is between 43 to 79 degrees Fahrenheit. Any dill caught outside during frost will die.

- **Feeding**

  Dill doesn't need much encouragement to grow and many herb gardeners will tell you that it does not need to be fertilized. I never fertilize my dill plants. I just make sure they have plenty of organic material mixed through their soil.

Pruning and harvesting dill

You should prune the top of your dill plants regularly, especially if buds form. This will ensure that the plant will continue to produce leaves over a long period. I prefer to harvest my dill in the morning as the moisture content in the leaves is at its highest and provides a stronger flavor to the herb. Of course, take leaves of the tree whenever you need them.

If you want more dill plants, wait for a plant to flower and then harvest the seeds off it. These can now grow more plants from these. If your dill plant is outside you can even leave it and let nature take its course. I guarantee you will have more dill plants in your garden the following year!

Preserving and storing dill

Dill can be left in the refrigerator for two to three days. I have so much dill in my garden that I never have to keep any excess leaves I might have harvested.

Dill leaves can also be dried, although I never use the dried variety, I just find fresh herbs so much better. To dry dill leaves, place them on waxed paper and leave in a nice dark area that has some warmth to it as well as air circulation. The leaves will dry out over a period of time and can be crumbled into a powder. Store this powder in an air tight container.

Dill can also be frozen in freezer bags or added to water, turned into ice and then kept in freezer bags.

Using dill in cooking

Of course, one of the best uses of dill is by adding them to pickles. Who can resist a dill pickle? The herb is far more versatile however. It can be used to help flavor stews, sauces, soups, casseroles, various pastas and meat or fish dishes. The French even use dill in their baking.

I love simple quick cooking and my favorite dill recipe is dill and cucumber dip. This really is so easy and packed full of lovely dill flavor. You will need the following ingredients.

- Medium cucumber

- White pepper (¼ teaspoon)
- Fresh dill (2 tablespoons, chopped)
- Mayonnaise (1 ½ cups)
- Sour cream (¾ cup)
- Green bell pepper (¼ cup, finely diced).

The rest is easy, mix everything together thoroughly and you have the most fresh tasting dip imaginable.

Other uses for dill

Dill has many different uses.

- Dill can be used to encourage sleep. If you have trouble sleeping, mix dill leaves with some hot milk and drink. This is a sleep remedy used in India.
- Dill water has been used over the centuries for babies with colic.
- Dill can also be used to fight indigestion and other stomach problems including diarrhea.
- Dill can be used to provide relief for sore eyes. Take dill seeds, submerge them in boiling water from 2 minutes. Allow to cool and place over the eyes with cotton wool. Leave them for twenty minutes and your eyes will feel better.

Dill can be used to freshen your breath.

OREGANO

Native to the Mediterranean region, oregano is from the origanum family and is a perennial herb. It grows between 8 and 32 inches tall and produces leaves up to 1.5 inches long. Oregano plants produce small, purple flowers.

People often get oregano and marjoram confused and although they have a number of similarities, they do have distinct tastes. Oregano has a strong, spicy flavor.

How to grow oregano

Although a fairly easy plant to grow, there are still a number of factors to consider when growing oregano.

- **Light**

  For outdoor plants you will want your oregano to be exposed to sunlight for at least half of the day. This helps to improve both its smell and give the plant very bright flowers. It can be grown in partial shade however. Be extremely careful in very hot climates as the herbs leaves can scorch. I like to let my outdoor plants receive early morning sunlight followed by partial shade.

  Indoor plants should ideally be left in an area that receives plenty of natural light. As with all my herbs, I like to place them near a window in my kitchen. Not only beneficial to them, but they are in close proximity when I cook.

- **Water**

  Oregano is very similar to all the other herbs we have mentioned so far. It cannot be overwatered at all so make sure indoor plants are allowed to drain properly. This is the key to healthy oregano plants. The herb itself can actually tolerate drier conditions for a time and well established plants are drought tolerant. Oregano plants do not like high humidity at all but will thrive in lower humidity areas.

Indoor plants should only be watered when the soil is dry. Then the plant should receive a good watering and be allowed to drain fully.

- **Soil**

In their natural habitat, oregano grow in fairly rocky terrain. Obviously this is difficult to replicate at home, but a loamy soil with some gravel to encourage drainage should be perfect.

For indoor plants, drainage is again crucial. I use a mix of potting soil, sand, perlite and peat moss in equal parts for my containers. It seems to work very well as my indoor plants thrive.

- **Temperature**

Temperature wise, oregano grow extremely well in the range of 55 – 70 degrees Fahrenheit. This applies to both indoor and outdoor plants. If you live in extremely cold regions you will not have much luck with this herb.

- **Feeding**

Oregano can be fertilized with a number of organic materials including fish meal, bone meal or worm casings. This is beneficial during the growing months and should be done at least once a month. You can also use normal granular or liquid fertilizer at a ratio 10:10:10. Do not feed the plant too much nitrogen as its leaves will increase in size, but also become far less flavorful.

Pruning and harvesting oregano

Oregano plants should be pruned every now and again. This helps both air circulation around the plant and can prevent diseases. For outdoor plants, pruning is useful if they become too bunched together. Also prune any area of the plant that might be showing distress.

Indoor plants can be pruned often as it stimulates growth. Do this by cutting the plants to around 3 inches in height (for smaller plants) and around 6 inches in height (for bigger plants).

The best time to harvest oregano is just before it starts to form flowers. This will give leaves with the strongest flavor. Once you have done this, cut the plant down to encourage it to grow again. Oregano can be harvested throughout the season.

Preserving and storing oregano

Oregano is an excellent herb to preserve through drying. This is because the plant still maintains its flavor throughout the drying process. Dried oregano also smells divine. There are a number of ways to dry out the herb.

Hang bunches in a cool, dry place such as an attic. Here the herb will dry out naturally, especially if you live in an area of low humidity. If you live in an area of higher humidity you may need to finish off the drying process by placing the herb on a baking sheet and leaving it in an open oven heated to around 200 degrees Fahrenheit. Do not leave the oven on! Once it has reached temperature you must turn it off. When the leaves are dry, remove them from the stem and store in a dark cupboard in glass jars.

The herb can also be frozen by blending the leaves together with some olive oil. It can then be placed in a freezer bag in the freezer.

Using oregano in cooking

What would pasta sauce be without oregano? It can be a great addition to many dishes including cabbage, mushrooms, zucchini, beans, tomatoes, peppers, eggplant, potatoes and many meat, poultry and seafood dishes. Dried oregano can also be used as a substitute for salt.

One of my favorite uses for all my fresh oregano is this simple bruschetta. Not only is it tasty, but it takes five minutes to make. You will need the following ingredients.

- Garlic (1 clove)
- Extra virgin olive oil (3 tablespoons, separated)
- Large, ripe tomatoes (4, diced)
- Red onion (½ cup diced)
- Fresh basil leaves (12, ripped or chopped)
- Fresh oregano leaves (2 tablespoons, chopped)
- Balsamic vinegar (1 tablespoon)
- Mozzarella cheese (½ cup, grated)
- Salt to taste
- Bruschetta (8 slices, ¾ inch thick)

Begin by toasting the bread in the oven. Take garlic and rub once side of the bread followed by a drizzle of olive oil. In a bowl, mix the tomatoes, onions, oregano, basil, olive oil (2 tablespoons), balsamic vinegar, salt and pepper. Spread this mixture over each slice of toast and then top with grated mozzarella. Place in a heated oven until the cheese begins to melt. Serve and enjoy!

Other uses for oregano

Oregano has many different uses.

- Dried oregano can be used in crafts.

- Oregano can be used to make some dyes.
- Oregano is used in a number of medicinal ways in Crete. These include toothache, stomach cramps and to ease tonsillitis. The easiest way to ingest oregano is as tea, either made from fresh or dried leaves. Place 1 to 2 teaspoons in hot water. Allow it to stand for 10 minutes and drink. This can be ingested up to three times per day.
- Oregano oils, obtained from its leaves can be used to treat athlete's foot.
- Oregano oils are used in soaps.
- Oregano makes excellent ground cover for the garden.

MARJORAM

Marjoram hails from Cyprus and Turkey. The leaves of this perennial plant are oval in shape, but fairly elongated. They are normally 0.2 to 0.5 inches in length and grow off a woody stem at alternate intervals. The plant produces small flowers along the stem in various colors but often lilac or white.

Marjoram and oregano, although very similar, are often confused as the same plant. They have very different tastes. Marjoram has a distinct pine and citrus flavors.

How to grow marjoram

Marjoram is a fairly hardy plant able to grow in tough conditions. You will need to consider the following.

- **Light**

  Marjoram grown outdoors prefers full sunlight. As with many of the other herbs I have mentioned, the sun cannot be too harsh. If it is, rather allow the plant to get morning sun and shade from midday onwards.

  Marjoram plants are more than happy to grow indoors if placed near natural light.

- **Water**

  Marjoram should be watered whenever the soil it is planted in shows signs of dryness. Do not overwater and allow the plant to drain properly. Unlike oregano, marjoram plants are not drought resistant, therefore check every day to see if it needs to be watered.

- **Soil**

  Marjoram grows extremely well in loamy soil. Ensure that it drains well, especially for indoor plants where the surface area around the herb is very small.

- **Temperature**

  Marjoram is not as hardy as oregano but will grow extremely well in the temperature range of 62 – 75 degrees Fahrenheit.

- **Feeding**

  Fertilizing marjoram depends completely on the quality of your soil. If it is poor, mix through some organic matter to feed your plant. If the soil quality is high, you can fertilize your plants before every growing season.

Pruning and harvesting marjoram

Pruning your marjoram plant will help to stimulate new growth. Remove all the older branches as well as those not producing leaves. Outdoor plants can be pruned to thin them out as well.

Marjoram should be harvested before they flower as the leaves become bitter afterwards. You could also choose to remove the flowers which will encourage the plant to grow even more. Leaves removed before flowering have the highest concentration of oils and taste the strongest.

Preserving and storing marjoram

Marjoram can be preserved through drying in a similar way to oregano.

Hang bunches in a cool, dry place with excellent ventilation. The herb will take some time to dry but if you live in an area of low humidity this is the perfect way to dry it out. If you live in an area of high humidity, you could dry the herb out in an oven set at 150 to 200 degrees

Fahrenheit. Once the oven has reached temperature, place the leaves inside on a baking tray, turn off the oven and leave the door open. Dried leaves can be stored in an air-tight container.

The herb can also be frozen by blending the leaves together with some olive oil. It can then be placed in a freezer bag in the freezer.

Using marjoram in cooking

Marjoram gives an excellent citrus zing and is a great addition in salads, sauces, gravy and when used in meat, fish and chicken dishes. It can also be used to help spruce up regular side dishes including this carrot dish. You will need the following ingredients.

- Olive oil (3 tablespoons)
- Garlic (1 clove, minced)
- Carrots (16 cut into diagonal ½ inch slices)
- Sugar (1 teaspoon)
- Salt (½ teaspoon)
- Black pepper (1/4 teaspoon)
- Fresh marjoram (1 tablespoon, chopped)
- Lemon juice (4 teaspoons)

In a frying pan heat half of the olive oil at a low heat. Add the following: garlic, carrots, sugar, half of the salt and the pepper. Cover and cook for around five minutes, stir occasionally. Remove the cover and continue to cook while raising the temperature to a moderate heat. Let the carrots start to brown and cook for a further 8 minutes. Once the carrots are tender, remove from the heat and add the remaining olive oil, salt, marjoram and lemon juice. Mix through and serve.

Other uses for marjoram

Marjoram is filled with antioxidants. It can be used in a tea format and drank to help to:

- Improve digestion.
- Improve appetite.
- Relieve nausea.
- Ease stomach cramps.
- Relieve diarrhoea and constipation.
- Fight fever.
- Relieve headaches.

MINT

Mint is found in various forms in a number of areas including Asia, Australia, North America, Africa and Europe. Mint plants are perennial with branch-like stems. The leaves appear in opposite pairs on each stem and are often oblong in shape with serrated edges. Depending on the type of mint, leaves are found in various colors including dark green, blue and purple. Mint produces small white flowers. The plant itself grows up to 45 inches in height.

How to grow mint

Mint grows very easily. In fact, in some areas it is considered an invasive plant. Let's look at a few factors that will influence the growth of mint in your herb garden or indoors.

- **Light**

  Mint plants love sun! They can thrive in full sunlight as long as it is not too harsh. If you live in an area with high temperatures, rather have your mint plants receive half a day sunlight either in the morning or afternoon. The plant can stay in shade for the other period of time.

  Indoor mint plants should be placed near a natural source of light such as a window.

- **Water**

  I am starting to sound like a stuck record but when it comes to watering herbs but as with the others I have mentioned, do not overwater mint! Mint plants, as with other herbs do not like to be left in standing water as this results in rot.

The plant should be watered when the top layer of soil is dry to the touch. Remember that humidity plays a big role in how often a plant may need to be watered. Plants in areas of low humidity will need to be watered far more often than those in a high humidity area. Soil quality can also play a role. If the mint is in very sandy soil, it will drain quickly and not hold any moisture, therefore you may have to water more often.

- **Soil**

Mint loves soil that holds moisture while providing excellent drainage. Loamy soil is a great option to grow you mint in. Adding a layer of mulch to poor quality soil can help it retain moisture. Indoor mint plants can use a mix that includes peat and perlite as well as organic materials.

- **Temperature**

Mint will grow very well if kept in a temperature range of between 54 and 84 degrees Fahrenheit. The plants growth will slow in temperatures higher than this.

- **Feeding**

Fertilize your mint with a standard 10-10-10 fertilizer mixed on to about half of its regular strength. This can be done just before growing season to give the plants a boost.

Pruning and harvesting mint

Pruning is only a necessity if the center of the plant becomes overcrowded. Cut back stems and branches to avoid different plants growing into each other. This is especially true of mint plants growing outside.

Mint should be harvested before the plants flower. Do this by cutting near the base of the stem, around 1 inch from the soil. Normally, a mint plant can be harvested up to three times each growing season. Alternatively, pick the leaves as you need them.

If you have mint in excess it can be both dried and frozen. However, these are both never better than fresh leaves!

To dry mint either hang the stems with leaves attached in a cool, dry place or you can place them on a tray and let them dry naturally. Of course, high humidity levels means your mint won't dry out so in that case, you can freeze the leaves in freezer bags and take out your fridge when needed.

Dried mint should be stored in air tight containers and will keep for up to a year.

Using mint in cooking

Mint has so many excellent uses in the kitchen in sauces, stews, teas and even ice-cream. Perhaps my favorite way to use fresh mint is in mint jelly. Drizzled over lamb… just heaven! To make an easy mint jelly you will need the following:

- Mint leaves and stems (1 cup)
- Apple cider vinegar (½ cup)
- Water (1 cup)
- Sugar (3½ cups) – Don't worry this recipe makes 2 pints!
- Food coloring (4 drops. This is optional).
- Liquid fruit pectin (3 ounces)

Bruise the mint leave and stems using a roller to ensure they release their flavor. Add them to a saucepan, then add the vinegar, water and sugar. Turn up the heat to high and let the ingredients boil, continue stirring so that the sugar melts. Now add the coloring (optional), followed by the fruit pectin. Bring the ingredients back to the boil and let it continue for around 30 seconds. Remove and skim any impurities off the surface. Pass the liquid through a very fine sieve and into piping hot, sterilized jelly jars. Seal, let it cool down and refrigerate.

Using mint in cooking

Mint can be used in a number of different ways.

- Mint (and spearmint in particular) are a natural pest repellant. Both aphids and ants cannot stand spearmint. Use spearmint in your garden to ward off these pests.
- Mint can also be planted near cabbage, broccoli and kohlrabi to help repel cabbage fly and cabbage looper.
- Mint also attracts insects that are beneficial to other garden plants.
- Mint can be used to repel fleas. Place two parts spearmint, one part thyme and one part fresh wormwood in a piece of material, seal and leave under your pet's bed and blankets.
- Peppermint tea can help soothe an upset stomach.
- Mint can help stop hiccups. Add mint leaves, a squeeze of fresh lemon juice and some salt to a glass of lukewarm water. Mix thoroughly and drink and your hiccups will disappear.
- Mint can be used as a quick breath freshener.

Mint is used in toothpastes and mouth-wash.

PARSLEY

Even those who do not use many herbs in their cooking know what parsley is! It is a herb that has been used through the ages, especially in the Mediterranean region, where it originated. Parsley comes in a number of varieties, but the most common used in cooking is flat leaf parsley.

Parsley can be grown as an annual plant. It is bright green in color and forms rosettes of leaves which can be as large as 4 inches in size. In the second year of growth the plant can produce flowers which generally are yellow-green in color. It can grow as high as 36 inches.

How to grow parsley

Parsley is a really easy herb to grow. You will need to control the following factors. If you do, you will have lush parsley bushes in your garden!

- **Light**

As it comes from the sunny Mediterranean region of Europe, parsley does not mind sunlight at all. The plant will require around 4-8 hours of sunlight every day and can withstand full sun. I tend not to let my parsley plants receive the harshest sun of the day, so as for most of my herbs, my parsley gets morning sun followed by afternoon shade.

- **Water**

Parsley plants have a long tap root that will go out in search of water. This root can grow very deep so ensure that you water your outdoor plants enough. I generally have to water my parsley plants once per week, but I do check daily. In hot weather, this might change to twice a week, depending on how long the weather holds for.

Indoor plants should be checked daily as they can dry out much quicker. Remember you will have to water the plant thoroughly but let all the excess water drain away.

- **Soil**

    For outside parsley plants loamy soil is best. You can also consider mulching around the plant to ensure poor soil remains moist. Either grass clippings that have been dried or finely chopped pine bark will make an excellent mulch. For indoor plants, you only need to ensure that the soil retains moisture but drains properly.

- **Temperature**

    Parsley will grow very well if kept in a temperature range of between 50 and 70 degrees Fahrenheit. Its growth is slowed when temperatures drop below 45 and rises above 75.

- **Feeding**

    Parsley can be fertilized, either by working organic material through the soil or by using commercial fertilizers such as a 5 - 10-5 vegetable variant. This can be applied during the middle of the growing season. For indoor plants, fertilizing can happen more frequently, as often as every six weeks in fact using the above-mentioned fertilizer, but at half strength.

Pruning and harvesting parsley

New parsley plants can be pruned when the plant itself reaches around 8 inches. Cut the outer leaves of the plant right to the ground to encourage growth. These outer leaves mature the quickest. Remember to remove any yellowing leaves.

Parsley can be harvested as needed, but start from the outside in and only when leaves have three fully formed segments. If you need the whole plant, cut all the stems at close to ground level.

Parsley can be stored in a refrigerator by placing it in a bowl of water. The herb can also be dried very successfully. The easiest method is to hang cut sprigs in an area that is ventilated, dry, warm but shady. Once dried out, crumbled the leaves and leave in an air tight container.

Parsley can also be frozen both by placing leaves in a freezer bag or by cutting them, combining with water and freezing in ice trays. Remove the ice and place in a freezer bag.

Using parsley in cooking

Parsley is a great addition to any soup, adding a real depth of flavor. The herb is also used in sauces, stews and casseroles and don't forget, as a garnish! Try this delicious potato and parsley soup. You will need the following ingredients.

- Peeled potatoes (1½ pounds)
- Parsley root (2, cleaned)
- Olive oil (1½ tablespoons)
- Onion (chopped finely)
- Bay leaves (2)
- White wine (⅓ cup)
- Parsley (2 cups chopped flat leaf)
- Salt
- Black pepper
- Vegetable stock (6 cups)
- Cream (⅓ cup)

Cut the potatoes into quarters lengthwise. Grate up the parsley root. Add the oil to your soup pot (on a medium heat), add the onions, potato, parsley root and bay leaves. Cook for around 7 minutes, occasionally stirring. Increase the heat, add the wine and reduce the liquid. Then add the parsley (leaving ½ a cup), vegetable stock and salt to taste. Let the soup begin to boil and then lower the heat to achieve a simmer. Leave the pot partially covered and cook until the potatoes break up. Stir in the cream and left-over parsley, add the pepper and serve!

Other uses for parsley

Parsley has a number of medicinal uses.

- Parsley juice fights eye infections and can be used to heal conjunctivitis.
- Parsley can be used as a natural diuretic.
- Parsley eases bladder infections.
- Rub bruised parsley leaves on insect bites to relieve itching.
- Parsley lowers blood pressure.

The easiest way to ingest parsley is in a tea form. This can be done with dried parsley by adding two tablespoons to eight ounces of water, mix and then boil for a period of 5 minutes to infuse all the flavors. Your parsley tea is now ready to drink.

ROSEMARY

Rosemary hails from the Mediterranean region, specifically North Africa, Greece, Portugal, Spain, Italy and the south of France. It is often found in rocky hills near the seaside where it grows in abundance. It has been used as both a medicinal and culinary herb in the area for centuries and was transported to Britain by the Romans in around the 8th Century.

Rosemary can grow to a height of between 24 and 72 inches. It has spiky green leaves which grow in abundance along its branches. They often have a greyish tint underneath. It can produce flowers which are a pale blue color.

How to grow rosemary

Rosemary is a fairly hardy herb that grows very well without too much attention once you have established the plant. To do that, take care of the following factors.

- **Light**

  Rosemary likes a lot of sun as well as humid environments. The plant can receive full sunlight for most of the day when kept outside. Indoor plants should be near a natural light source at all times, either a skylight or a large window.

- **Water**

  The herb requires very little water once it is a mature plant. It does not need to be watered as often as others and should not be planted in a moist area of your garden. Having said that, you should still check the plant regularly and water when needed. Indoor plants can be placed in terracotta pots which will also help to absorb any excess water.

- **Soil**

  Rosemary plants grow naturally in rocky areas, often in spots with sandy soil. This herb does not mind a well-draining sandy soil. I prefer to work some gravel through the soil as well as to try to simulate its natural environment as much as possible.

- **Temperature**

  Rosemary can tolerate very hot temperatures but colder temperatures below 30 degrees Fahrenheit will affect the plant negatively and can kill it. If you live in colder conditions, rather keep outdoor plants in pots that can be moved to a warmer area on cold nights.

- **Feeding**

  I like to add a fertilizer to the soil of my outdoor plants especially when they are young. I use a slow-release variety as this is perfect to boost the young plants as they grow. You can also use this kind of fertilizer on indoor rosemary plants.

Pruning and harvesting rosemary

Remove any broken branches from the plant as well as any yellowing leaves. The best time to harvest your rosemary plant is just before it flowers as the herb will have its strongest flavor at this point. Harvesting should only begin in the second year after planting as this allows the plant to establish itself fully.

Of course, if you need a few leaves here and there you can snip them off the plant at any time although you should not harvest while it is in bloom.

Rosemary is the perfect herb to dry. Hang long stems of the herb in a dark area of your house that has excellent air circulation and warmth to encourage the herb to dry out. The herb will retain its green color and once dried can be pounded down into a powder.

Rosemary can also be frozen but has a tendency to go black. One way to overcome this is to cover with a thin coating of olive oil and place in a freezer bag. Alternatively, place chopped leaves into an ice tray with olive oil, freeze and then place the olive oil blocks in a freezer bag.

Using rosemary in cooking

Many Italian dishes make use of Rosemary including roast meats. Rosemary is also often used with other dishes including meats, fish, shellfish, potato, carrot, onions, soups, stews and sauces. I love to use sprigs of rosemary as a basting brush for when I am roasting meat. This allows a subtle flavor to permeate the meat. Perhaps my favorite use of the herb is in this roast potato dish. You will need the following ingredients.

- Peeled potatoes (7 medium)
- Salt (2 teaspoons, separated)
- Cornmeal (2 tablespoons)
- Black pepper (½ teaspoon)
- Olive oil (¾ cup)
- Rosemary (2 sprigs worth of leaves, minced up)
- Peeled garlic (8 cloves)

Set your oven to 425 degrees Fahrenheit. Place a rack at the lowest level to warm. Quarter your potatoes and add to a pot of cold water with 1 teaspoon of salt. Bring to a boil, turn down the heat a little and continue to boil for 2 minutes. In a bowl, mix the cornmeal, the remaining salt and black pepper. Place the drained potatoes into the cornmeal mixture and toss through. Be gentle so as not to break the potatoes up. Heat the olive oil in a very heavy pan. Add the rosemary and garlic once the oil is very hot. This will infuse it with the flavors of these two ingredients. Add the potatoes, arranging them evenly. Now place the pan in the oven and roast for 15 minutes at which point you remove it and turn the potatoes over. Continue to roast for around 20 minutes or until all the potatoes are golden.

Other uses for rosemary

Rosemary can be used in many other ways, many of them medicinal in nature.

- Rosemary oil can be used by people suffering with arthritis. Rub the oil on the infected areas daily.
- Rosemary oil will also heal bruises.
- Rosemary oil can also treat dandruff. Apply to the scalp, leave for around an hour and wash with shampoo.
- Rosemary makes an excellent air freshener. Simmer a pot of water with rosemary, 1 slice of a citrus fruit and some vanilla. The incredible smell will permeate your house.

SAGE

As with many other herbs, Sage is found in the Mediterranean, but this time specifically the northern coast, including Yugoslavia. The herb is one of the main exports of the country and more than half the sage produced in the world comes from this area including Croatia, Montenegro and Albania. It is a great culinary herb but also used for medicinal purposes in fact, history shows that it was never even used as a culinary herb by the Romans. It seemed to start to be used for cooking around the 16th Century in Europe.

Sage plants grow to around 30 inches tall. They have long leaves that are fairly narrow. These leaves are gray green in color and feel rough to the touch. The plant produces mauve, pink, purple and white flowers. There are many varieties of sage available.

How to grow sage

Sage is a fairly resilient plant and easy to grow in a home environment.

- **Light**

  Sage plants do not shy away from the sunlight. Outdoor plants can be planted in areas that receive between 6 – 8 hours of sunlight per day, although a period of shade will not harm the plant. Too much shade however, will cause the plant to begin to droop. Indoor plants will grow quite happily in close proximity to a natural light source such as a large window.

- **Water**

  As with many of the herbs I have previously described, Sage should be watered fairly often. It is imperative that the water is able to drain away from the plant otherwise rot can set in. Indoor plants will dry out quicker than those outside and should be watered more often. Obviously conditions vary from location to location and plants should be checked often.

- **Soil**

  Sage plants demand a soil that drains well. A loamy soil often works best for the plants as it has the ability to drain while holding the correct moisture content. This ensures that the plant does not go thirsty. If outdoor soil conditions are not ideal, consider using mulching around the plants to help retain some moisture.

- **Temperature**

  As a fairly hardy plant, I have found sage to grow in wide range of temperatures. Its ideal range is between 60 – 80 degrees Fahrenheit, although it will tolerate colder night time temperatures of around 40 degrees Fahrenheit. This will cause growth to slow.

- **Feeding**

  When it comes to feeding Sage, I tend to give new plants a boost as soon as I have planted them. I just use a normal, standard fertilizer which seems to work very well. Remember not to overfeed the plant.

Pruning and harvesting sage

Sage plants generally have a 4 to 5 year life span. After this period their leaves start to lose their flavor and become very woody. By pruning the plant, the herb will grow even more.

The plant can be pruned after it has flowered. Normally, I cut the plant down to half its size, starting with the larger, woodier stems. Remove any parts of the plant that are damaged or broken. Never prune to a level lower than where the leaves end.

Sage leaves can be harvested at any time they are required. If you are wanting a large batch to dry, harvest the plant just before flowers start to form. Sage leaves are easy to dry and retain much of their flavor. They can be dried in bunches in a warm, dry, shaded area with excellent air circulation. Individual leaves can also be dried in this manner. Place them on a wax paper and leave them. Once they have dried, crunch them up and seal them in an air tight container.

Sage can also be frozen. Place whole leaves in freezer bags in your freezer. Use in cooking as required.

Using sage in cooking

The flavor of sage compliments a number of dishes. It goes well with a number of meats including lamb, veal, game, duck, fish, pork and many others. Of course, one of the most famous uses for the herb is in poultry stuffing. What would Thanksgiving turkey be without stuffing! Try this delicious recipe.

- Butter (4 tablespoons)
- Onion (1 medium, chopped)
- Celery stalks (3, cut in ¼ inch slices)
- Salt (½ teaspoon)
- Ground sage (1 teaspoon)
- Dried Thyme (1 teaspoon)
- Dry bread cut into cubes / croutons (10 cups)
- Chicken stock (1½ cups)
- Egg (1, whisked)

Set your oven to 350 degrees Fahrenheit. Take a large pan and begin to melt the butter. Begin cooking the onions, celery, sage, thyme and salt on a medium heat for around 5 minutes. Remove from the heat once done. Now place the bread/croutons into the onion mixture. Add the chicken broth, slowly fold the bread/croutons into the liquid and onions. Add a whisked egg while continuing to fold, mixing everything thoroughly. Place the mixture into an ovenproof dish and bake until crispy on top, around 40 minutes.

Other uses for sage

Sage is filled with anti-oxidants and can be used for many other things including:

- Sage leaves can be put into small cloth bags and left in cupboards throughout the house to repel moths.
- Sage tea can help to ease sore throats.
- Sage can be used as a disinfectant.
- Sage tea reduces menopausal night sweats.
- Sage tablets can stop excessive sweating.
- Sage can be used as a toner for people with oily skin.
- Sage leaves steeped in boiling water and cooled can be used to treat dandruff.

THYME

Thyme, another herb from the Mediterranean region was used in many ancient cultures. The Egyptians used the herb as part of the embalming process while in Greece formed part of religious ceremonies. The Romans are believed to have spread the herb through their conquests. They used it to flavor food, specifically cheese and certain drinks.

The thyme plant itself takes the form a small shrub. It has a very pungent smell and produces flowers that are pink, lavender and sometimes white. The leaves of the plant are very small and a grayish green color. There are many species of the plant but perhaps the most famous is English thyme used in culinary circles. Other varieties including lemon and caraway thyme.

How to grow thyme

Now I could make a joke here about it taking time to grow thyme, but I won't! The plant grows very well in a number of locations as long as you factor in the following considerations.

- **Light**

  Thyme prefers sunlight, the more the better. There is no need for the plant to have any shade, but a few hours will not cause any harm. Indoor plants must be kept near a source of natural light.

- **Water**

  Thyme plants do need to be watered on a fairly regular schedule. They prefer the soil to have some moisture, but do not overwater! Indoor plants should be checked often. When watered, they should be allowed to drain thoroughly.

- **Soil**

Thyme grows extremely well in loamy soil, although most soil types can support the plant as long as it receives enough water.

- **Temperature**

  Thyme grows best in a moderate climate, but can survive colder temperatures. An optimal temperature range is 59 – 77 degrees Fahrenheit.

- **Feeding**

  Thyme does not need fertilizer during the growing season, however I like to give my thyme plants a little boost just before. A general all-purpose fertilizer is more than sufficient for the task.

Pruning and harvesting thyme

Like any other woody herb, Thyme benefits from an occasional pruning as this encourages more growth. Pruning also prevents the plant from becoming too woody which eventually causes its leaves to lose flavor. To prune the plant, cut back the older stems by about two-thirds. Remove any broken branches whenever you find them on the plant.

Thyme can be harvested as needed. If you are wanting to harvest a large batch for drying, this should be done before the plant flowers. With small leaves that grow in bunches, Thyme lends itself to drying. Similar to other woody herbs, this is achieved by hanging bunches of the plant in a cool, dark, well-ventilated area. After a while, they would have dried and can be crumbled and kept in air tight containers.

The herb can also be frozen using the ice cube method. Add thyme leaves to water in ice trays and freeze. Remove the ice cubes and store in freezer bags to be used when needed. Alternatively, cover the thyme leaves in a thin coating of olive oil and place in freezer bags to use when required.

Using thyme in cooking

Thyme is used in many Mediterranean styled dishes and works very well with eggs, vegetables, pork, game, lamb and some fish. It is also an essential ingredient of the famed bouquet garni, a collection of herbs used in French cooking, specifically in the region of Provence. Try this excellent side dish of green beans with thyme. You will need the following ingredients.

- Fresh green beans (2 pounds)
- Butter (½ stick)
- Dijon mustard (1 tablespoon)
- Garlic salt (1 teaspoon)
- Thyme (2 tablespoons, chopped)
- Toasted almonds (⅓ cup, slivered)

Start off by cooking your beans in a large pot of boiling water. Be sure to add salt to taste. They should be cooked until they still have some crunch but approaching tender. Drain the water off the beans and plunge them into a bowl of ice water. This stops them from cooking immediately and allows them to keep their color. Drain the beans. Melt the butter in a large pan over a medium to high temperature. Add half the thyme, mustard and garlic and mix through the butter. Now add the beans, ensuring they are coated by the butter mixture. Allow them to heat through. Place them in a serving bowl and sprinkle with the left-over thyme and the almonds.

Other uses for thyme

Thyme is found in a number of modern products including mouthwash and hand sanitizers.

- Thyme can lower blood pressure. Use it as a substitute for salt.
- Thyme tea can ease coughing.
- Thyme can boost the immune system.

- Thyme can be used as a disinfectant.
- Thyme rubbed on the skin can repel mosquitoes.

CONCLUSION

I hope you have enjoyed reading through this book.

Herbs really can be used for some many different things. The great thing about them though is that they are very easy to grow, perfect for beginner gardeners.

Let's be honest, what can be better than stepping out to your own garden and harvesting a few herbs to add to your evening meal.

If you have never had a herb garden, perhaps the best place to start is with a few herbs that you can grow indoors, preferably by the kitchen window. I would suggest rosemary, basil and thyme. They are fairly forgiving and can also be used in a wide range of foods.

Once you gain a little more experience, you can always start with a bigger herb garden outside. Who knows, eventually you might be growing all 10 of the herbs I have mentioned here.

Remember, do not be afraid to take that first step. You will be pleasantly surprised to find how much fun growing herbs can be.

Happy gardening!

RESOURCES

The following websites will help further your knowledge on growing herbs.

- Bouquet Garni Herb Site
  http://herb.co.za/start-your-own-herb-garden/

- Better Home and Garden
  http://www.bhg.com/gardening/vegetable/herbs/easy-to-grow-herbs/

- Planet Natural
  http://www.planetnatural.com/herb-gardening/

- Herb Info
  http://www.herbinfosite.com/

- Succulents and Sunshine
  http://www.succulentsandsunshine.com/succulent-care/

- Herb Gardening.com
  http://herbgardening.com/index.htm

ABOUT THE AUTHOR

Louise Harvey has been gardening for most of her life. She initially spent time in the garden to be close to her mother, but it wasn't long before she had got the bitten by the gardening bug herself.

Her mother gave her a corner of the garden to look after and she used her patch to grow flowers and vegetables. Once she had used up all of the space, she started filling up her bedroom with house plants and taking over the rest of the family home. Louise's mum gradually gave me more space to work with in the garden and eventually shared the entire backyard with her.

She hasn't stopped since. The main difference now is that she has her own home and garden to work on, and her mother has her own one back.

Louise vows to continue learning and experimenting in the garden for as long as possible. She enjoys trying out new methods for optimal growth and isn't afraid to make mistakes along the way. She confesses to making thousands of mistakes in her time in the garden, and she's keen to pass on what she's learned to amateur gardeners alike.

Gardening has changed her life forever. She finds it relaxing, fun, and hugely rewarding. She would like everyone to discover the same benefits.

She's helped numerous friends, family members and colleagues with their home and garden, and she wants to reach out to help more people. Her books are quick reference guides that are simple to understand, fun to read, and provide the amateur gardener with the basic information they need to start gardening.

OTHER BOOKS BY LOUISE HARVEY

Air Plants - A Beginners Guide To Understanding Air Plants, Growing Air Plants and Air Plant Care

Your First Orchid - A Beginners Guide To Understanding Orchids, Growing Orchids And Orchid Care

Your First Bonsai - A Beginners Guide To Bonsai Growing, Bonsai Care, and Understanding The Bonsai

Composting - The Complete Guide To Composting and Creating Your Own Compost

Self Sufficient Living - A Beginners Guide To Self Sufficient Living and Homesteading

14350006R00033

Printed in Great Britain
by Amazon.co.uk, Ltd.,
Marston Gate.